Pebble Plus

PET RABBITS

Questions and Answers

by Christina Mia Gardeski

This bo

The lo
a furt'

raintree

a Capstone company — publishers for children

Raintree is an imprint of Capstone Global Library Limited, a company incorporated in England and Wales having its registered office at 264 Banbury Road, Oxford, OX2 7DY – Registered company number: 6695582

www.raintree.co.uk
myorders@raintree.co.uk

Edited by Carrie Braulick Sheely and Michelle Hasselius
Designed by Kayla Rossow
Picture research by Pam Mitsakos
Production by Gene Bentdahl

ISBN 978 1 4747 2138 7 (hardback)
20 19 18 17 16
10 9 8 7 6 5 4 3 2 1

ISBN 978 1 4747 2150 9 (paperback)
21 20 19 18 17
10 9 8 7 6 5 4 3 2 1

British Library Cataloguing in Publication Data
A full catalogue record for this book is available from the British Library.

Every effort has been made to contact copyright holders of material reproduced in this book. Any omissions will be rectified in subsequent printings if notice is given to the publisher.

All the internet addresses (URLs) given in this book were valid at the time of going to press. However, due to the dynamic nature of the internet, some addresses may have changed, or sites may have changed or ceased to exist since publication. While the author and publisher regret any inconvenience this may cause readers, no responsibility for any such changes can be accepted by either the author or the publisher.

Acknowledgements
Alamy: ableimages, 17; Capstone: Gina Kammer, 19; iStockphoto: Susan Chiang, 21;
Shutterstock: Ana Aviskina, 1, 22, Cherkas, cover, MaxShutter, 15, Nadezda Murmakova, 7, Pe3k, 13, Pressmaster, 9;
Thinkstock: CBCK-Christine, 11, Fuse, 5

Printed and bound in China.

Contents

Who needs a friend? 4

Why do rabbits have long ears? 6

How well can rabbits see? 8

Why do rabbits twitch their noses? 10

What do rabbits eat? 12

Why do rabbits chew? 14

Can I train my rabbit? 16

Can I let my rabbit out of its cage? 18

How long do pet rabbits live for? 20

Glossary 22

Read more 23

Websites 23

Comprehension questions 24

Index 24

Who needs a friend?

My rabbit!

Rabbits love to be with

their owners or other rabbits.

They may sit with you. But they

don't always like to be held.

Why do rabbits have long ears?

A rabbit's ears help to keep it cool.

Blood cools as it flows through

the rabbit's long ears. Their ears

can also hear sounds

more than a kilometre away.

How well can rabbits see?

A rabbit has one eye on each

side of its head. Its eyes rotate.

A rabbit can see above and

behind without turning its head.

It cannot see in front of its nose.

Why do rabbits twitch their noses?

Rabbits may twitch their noses

more than 100 times a minute.

The twitches help rabbits to smell.

Rabbits smell food and other rabbits.

Pet rabbits remember your scent.

What do rabbits eat?

Rabbits are plant eaters.

Pet rabbits munch on hay and vegetables.

They also eat food called pellets.

Rabbits eat their own droppings.

They have vitamins that the rabbits need.

Why do rabbits chew?

Rabbits chew for fun and good health. Rabbits have 28 teeth. Their teeth never stop growing. Chewing hay helps to keep their teeth short.

Can I train my rabbit?

Some rabbits will follow commands.

You can train your rabbit to come

when called and do simple tricks.

Can I let my rabbit out of its cage?

Rabbits enjoy exercise. Make sure you have a rabbit run in the garden. Your rabbit can run around and play, but stay safe. If you have an indoor rabbit, you may let her run around indoors.

How long do pet rabbits live for?

Pet rabbits can live for 8 to 12 years.

Take your rabbit to a vet for

regular check-ups. Keep its

home clean. Good care keeps

rabbits happy and healthy.

Glossary

droppings animal waste

exercise activity done in order to stay healthy

pellet small, dry roll of rabbit food

rotate turn in a circle

scent smell of something

twitch make small, quick movements

vet person who cares for animals

vitamin something in food that is needed for good health

Read more

Bunny's Guide to Caring for your Rabbit (Pets' Guides), Anita Ganeri (Raintree, 2013)

Care for your Rabbits (RSPCA Pet Guide), RSPCA (HarperCollins, 2015)

Looking After Rabbits (Usborne Pet Guides), Fiona Patchett (Usborne Publishing, 2013)

Websites

www.dkfindout.com/uk/animals-and-nature/pet-care
Find out more about pet care.

www.rspca.org.uk/adviceandwelfare/pets/rabbits
Find out more about owning a rabbit.

Comprehension questions

1. Why do rabbits twitch their noses? Use the text to help you find your answer.

2. Rabbits eat pellets. What are pellets?

3. Rabbits can follow your commands and learn simple tricks. What trick would you teach your pet rabbit to do?

Index

ears 6
exercise 18
eyes 8
food 12, 14
hearing 6
life span 20

noses 8, 10
sense of smell 10
teeth 14
tricks 16
twitching 10
vets 20